Our Garden Diary

By Heather Hammonds

Photographs by Lyz Turner-Clark

Illustrations by Rachel Tonkin

Spring Time

One day,
Katie and I
made a little garden.
Aunty Sue helped us.

We made a garden diary, too.

Our
Garden
Diary

Week 1

We got
some little bean plants
from the garden shop.

We dug some holes
in our garden for the plants.

Week 2

We looked after
our little plants.

Katie watered them.

Week 4

Our little plants got bigger.
They had lots of new leaves.

Our plants looked very good.

Week 6

Aunty Sue saw a snail on a leaf.

The snail made a big hole
in the leaf.

Week 8

We saw some flowers
on our plants.

We looked

for some little beans.

Week 10

The beans on our plants got bigger and bigger.

Our plants had
lots of green beans.

Aunty Sue cooked the beans
for us.
We liked them.